Truitt has produced a site-specific poetry triangulated between the transcript of improvised language, snapshots, and the tenuous, tremulous breath of an embodied speaker. This poetry comes, that is, from the mete: "a particular point or position, esp. a turning point [verse, trope, corner] or finishing point [publication]." In doing so, Truitt twice *metes* urban space (travels over or traverses; paints or depicts) with a protocol that repeatedly *metes* (measures): "the space between your head and heart, trail of shadows among whispers," which is to say "the space between what you think and what you feel," "the oscillating intervals, felt as a throb, between wakefulness and sleep" (*mete*, in the obsolete intransitive impersonal, means "to dream"). Here at the boundary (*mete*) between speech and writing, word and image, the personal and the civic — here in this 21st-Century version of Personism — one can readily judge (*mete*) the extent (*mete*) to which Truitt truly meets the mark (*mete*: "also a mark or target. Also *fig.*").

—*Craig Dworkin*

VERTICAL ELEGIES 6:
STREET METE

Published by Station Hill Press, Inc., 124 Station Hill Road, Barrytown, NY 12507
www.stationhill.org

Station Hill of Barrytown literary publication is a project of The Institute for Publishing Arts, Inc., a not-for-profit, Federally tax-exempt organization (501(c)(3)) in Barrytown, New York.

Cover design by Susan Quasha.
Interior design by Sherry Williams, Oxygen Design Group, and Kathryn Weinstein.

Illustration: Kim Jaye, *Empire* (1998), mixed media on foamcore, 10 ¾ x 13 ¾ inches, private collection. Copyright 1998 Kim Jaye, all rights reserved.

The publisher and author thank the editors of the following venues where versions of and/or excerpts from these works originally appeared: *Barzakh; Coconut; Critophilia;* *88: A Journal of Contemporary American Poetry; Nedge; Paul Revere's Horse; Tool:* *A Magazine; Torch; UBUWEB; Western Humanities Review;* and *Wildlife.*

The author thanks The Fund for Poetry and the George A. and Eliza Gardner Howard Foundation for their support.

Library of Congress Cataloging-in-Publication Data

Truitt, Sam.
  Vertical elegies 6 : street mete / Sam Truitt.
     p. cm.
  ISBN 978-1-58177-121-3
  I. Title. II. Title: Vertical elegies six.
  PS3620.R85V48 2011
  811'.6--dc22
  2010045587

To Kim Jaye &
Michael Ruby

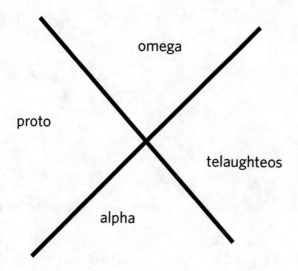

omega

proto

telaughteos

alpha

STREET
METE

CONTENTS

Raße æfter ßon
on fagne flor feond treddode...
—*Beowulf, 724-725*

tuesday, august 10, 1998

the wells at the mouth of itza

the sun is an orange chasm we are plunging   the jungle a flow a
single unifying key   continual earth crying storm   transcription
of lightning on water spout   a column of stone   we are ever
alone   the jungle's drooling thicket the edge of the clearing left
toilet paper purple flowers blue flowers crimson flowers and so i
have come to nothing banging a drum   beyond a road divides
underground between power failures jerking what the land goes
up from   there is a stone angle platforms the earth pushing
upward the land grizzled   attitude disappears   the sky disap-
pears   only the door into it remains   a phallus   someone is
singing hacking at earth with scythe   scale does not matter
    we do not matter   time doesn't matter though all is drawn in
it   though everything is yellow flowers   faces shine inwardly
building against them   silence is nothing   underground river
    do not believe anything   you will die   it is these splinters
10 levels to the sky   where the clouds lie   the stones are teeth
    there are no people   no place without a face   strangled in
geometry   always the sheath   there is a god at the top of the
stairs   there is one level   the stones are not teeth   this is not
a mouth   this is not a world it has swallowed   dispersion of
trees   a man sits alone under one   a thousand butterflies fling
themselves   one stone   one world   one block of ice under the
sun 4 interjects like a knife   already nothing is left to go inside
and die inside   feather   ochre sky   truth   ready now   where
few describe what is incised flame in debris   the shattered aba-
cus   here we felt   place your hand in your mouth   terraces of
mass and moss nobody is home to tell us how are you and not to
know but be and not to answer the question we are not enough to
figure here fiercer than water   space that has no face to say what
we feel blood drying some   not to climb but to be climbed   take
all the figures out   is this how it is really kind of crooked?   to
leave the road in the ruin   you are here   fresh oaks grass roots
roofs   pillars   the pillars   years   the years   what is above
and what is below   pillars trees time laid on their side   shad-
ows   we have left nothing   hide discus in diamond shape

a god sat here   if we had one thought they have left it   always
the face in the sun the disc of   human whistling in the jungle
terror is nothing   the moment observes walls that fill the space
between the columns   sky god emerging from the mouth of a ser-
pent higher than they are wide here that dug to live among
columns the knotting of the ears alongside the planet venus morn-
ing star an offering consisting of the skull of a decapitated man
found in the eastern stairwell   this is what we found   we found
we could do nothing   a hawk swings above   square pyramid hid-
ing circle of construction   there is a circle outside   guts her whole
roots with no tree   body with no heart   an iguana   rooms
square holes   breathe   jungle   peeked stone   chambers   pas-
sages   ways through   to bring it the darkness through you in
a chain of syllables   no place without a face   nothing to go
through   there is no way out   we must remember who we are

there is no place to stand   jaguar behind steel cage   cannot
stay. we cannot leave

saturday, june 5, 1999

—for TR

i wonder if we could unravel these details
would you lay down with me   these
insignificant things look back together and
understand   i see it everywhere on walls on
buildings at the end of history all illiadic
glossy hype   just a distraction from the city
which is her long hair something breathing
black trunks with the yellow oaks peripher-
al to the park   the b train splattered with
rain arrives at columbus circle so it must be
raining in the bronx   the big death parade
ontological and happy singing into my palm
 the big night that is my shepherd labor-
ing with the high smiths of thought to
construct something more   impressionis-
tic cock

60. Hear faintly car alarm grind a spot of fear into snow, distance enarmored by dominant honky culture.

92. Reflect with awe on the thought the life you live may be your own.

49. Watch the vales of shifting purple twilit clouds out her window as she relates the story of her father's "second letter."

87. Realize at Ruby's book party talking to Peter and Andy that the moment is the true indivisible unit of the world's economy on which to base human currency.

eclipse

        pinned again against the light the dark   mirror makes see
                  echo we   echo le' go my égo

        the smooth head of it

        the hole cut out   of the middle

        the riddle in the ruin   is tender

monday, february 3, 1997

before it begins there is the
space of its beginning   to
force one's self to the road to
the child held by one leg the
other arm under the shoulders
cradled there waiting for a yel-
low cab this boy in a red snow-
suit in the sunny morning

the sidewalks watered down
each morning now dry in the
sun   the poinsettia left on the
street stands outside the build-
ing on the 2nd of february

will it survive the night the
week the month? will someone
come take it in preserve it?

bill blass hates them spades
of red leaves scentless some
pacific shrub but it is alive never-
theless potted equipped to grow
its leaves still ruddy its whole
complexion giving off "it is not
it but us with our breath held"

6. Spend a half hour with
Ramon—maybe just 50 with a
handsome rugged face and
implacable air of kindness—
in Costa Rican Harlem hard-
ware shop basement precisely
cutting seven corners out of a
¾-inch plywood slab to ride
into your wall and thus form a
broad and frankly superlative
writing surface over which you
are now, data entering.

97. Surprise yourself when she asks
why you like the smell of sex by
saying it reminds you of where
we come from.

52. Feel winter smoke open your
throat as you lean into its
breath and reaching and
pulling back then into crouch
to spring the year in all its
wheels and marvels and lives
and disassociations of big
earth pistons bright with page,
sweet briar and Normandy
maple ahead.

eye

then our voices are who we are when we are most alone to hear them
teardrop in the shape of body
                                        in the shape of the light at the mouth of the
                        tunnel going down into darkness
man with propeller attached to chest prepares to dismember
    a number   a daddy-longlegs and flick it at the jury
                                                    the injury
hodehum walking between vales   of the exposed manhattan schist
            how real can it be   "we be"
                    wobbles   but we don't fall down
                        we be rock
            we be walking through the tunnel toward the zoo
toward you
            toward the smell of eglantine
a white world in a white moment
insect with a human face   rolling out of reach

forwarding this grace   but you have to lose your place

line in pirouette   the bottom line   the rounded crest
the body's pale horizon

saturday, november 18, 1995

white building in a smoke of
lights tiered though only its last
stories   against a dark block of
tenements in the night its height
hung over the city in white light
   orpheus is not a submarine but
a vision walked the city   each
human being also of constant
pain suppressed amid a process of
recollection

22. Awake to see the gray day gathered
around hexagonal granite tower and
wonder if this were war would one
emplace there a gun turret?

77. Drink a Corona at the Kamaka on 8th
amid its Christmas lights and Bob
Marley music with the sculptor Richter
preparing to return in four days to
Hamburg, relishing his perfect wise
journeyed profile pinioned between
hope and regret at leaving Manhattan.

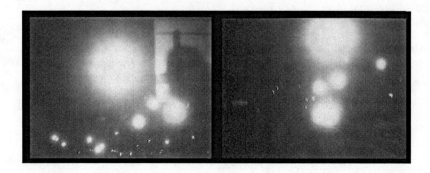

edge

"yeah, i'm gonna be the second"

                      i'm walking with aaron talking to his father talking
           to the spirit world
and everything is streaming out through a hole in our
selves
for lack of a better term
            does something come in   as everything goes out?
          "no, it's a man. edgar"
            & what would he have made of this   tree lit from below
from where the grave goes?
          walking down the street
            light empties them and light reflecting off them also
everything seems so simple.   does that mean stupid also?
          "say hi to my friend   sam?"

mouth 1

beyond a road divides underground between power failures
jerking what the land goes up from

we do not matter

it is these splinters 10 levels to the sky
where the clouds lie
                              we are only taking up what was left off
this is not a world it has swallowed

feather

space that has no face to say what we feel blood drying some

the pillars
                              we are only taking up what was left off
a god sat here

a hawk swings above
                                   a little overlap start as a point
square holes
                                   the worst of it over and above us
no place without a face

the jungle a flow a single unifying key
                              cool dead woman on a subway train

tuesday, december 22, 1998

gallery life in brooklyn, including art
& language

—for CC

life death fear. sack of shit   we are
never more one then when we are two
people joined through the sexes

    they are infinite on each the face of
santa   claus   walking   backward
through snowfall   on each flake the
face of santa claus emerging through
tunnel face distorted in oval mask
just as are all our impressions varia-
tions on happy birthday mr. presi-
dent   i went to a lot of trouble to
understand western civilization is
based on envy engendered by public-
ity   the publicity works upon anxi-
ety and the sum of everything is
money   to get money is to overcome
anxiety   publicity is the life of this
culture   without publicity capital-
ism flounders   these things i take to
bed at night sight glimpses of the
bend in the road ahead in the head a
road made of days we have brought
here to examine how to form a
thought that will not crumple parts
that fit and parts that turn to meet us
out ahead   blank space where my
body has been

13. Reflect with borrowed pride on
the Sugar Hill mansions chug-
ging up the sky in tough toast
of mornings' edges scenes of
dilapidation and exaltation.

134. Drop one by one in a mixture of
both pain and gladness all your
flirtations remembering Au-
gustine in love, finally, with one.

119. Measure the oscillating inter-
vals, felt as a throb, between
wakefulness and sleep and
know the surface on which
they play's your heart.

99. Think to drop to the basement
to check on your books and
between an unauthorized
move and the spring floods
discover one-tenth of your col-
lection as well as various
unique prints and memorabil-
ia, irrevocably ruined, will be
added—a sodden gray heavy
mass—to the weight of your
conscience.

130. Feel the dirt under your vest
as you poke at a hole in your
sweat.

hang

          the whole hero thing   delicious dangling
how to get purchase   making time with the   flies of restraint
holding off to hold on
so much metal
when did we become held in it   and if we are that are we each in our
own right   swordfighters
if the card is a sword
& the earring is a sword   or shield or whatever
metal against metal
music   rubber   life
          everywhere electricity speed
dangerous speed
        speed is salvation

speed is
        when you are dead where does it go?
speed is
        when you are alive where does it go?

        what is it to the lady with the pink hair
        a big ragged jagged   slab of

            holding my heart in

wednesday, july 17, 1996
hotel empire

it happens like that. you look up   in red neon against night sky a hole that's not named that anymore just all of us disappearing under assumed names poised above our lives big blocks of words that obscure the sky

nothing is written on their faces or everything is the big blocks that go against sky we can't roll   we walk around them by them blind   big blocks that absorb time   or nothing is written on our faces   so many within us so many without   the things in this city their feel & touch so many sounds do not fit in our mouths   we go unassuming through big blocks of sound

89. Meet Flo at the Hog Pit before showing at Stackhouse's gallery series to read Senator Byrd's speech beginning "Today I weep for my country."

26. Feel the calluses on the palms of thought and know them as words— and then wonder, "What are they holding?"

84. Swallow emptiness and despair.

36. Sit with her in the solarium under white imitation fur rug drinking coffee and discussing the conclusions of 19th century French novels.

29. Stop to watch workmen haul on a rope-and-trashcan system fresh cropper sheets to the roof of Convent Baptist Church.

light

        you & I & memory   lie
    between two hands   inviolately split

    the roar of torn pages open &   close
        the primordial flicker

to gasp   the words between the flames

tuesday, june 13, 2000

to see to really see the thought nothing
i can do   take a few breaths here
    the blinds are drawn across 23rd
on the maple tree growing to the
window like james schuyler   the
building is not so complicated from a
distance   blue sky   syllables

42. Spend the second day of the New Year
    reading the whole of Jack Black's *You
    Can't Win.*

82. Sense bats peen and knife through the
    ruined rafters of your mind.

23. Linger over the knowledge that anytime you
    feel the grease in your body glow is good.

brim

—for KJ

        something is burning   almost heaven
among dinky towns   among dinky mountain
tops of   appellation namely "the state of naming"
which is what worlds are   to be born
        name a few things   & then wander off
this page erected a moment

some scribble   some go cursive   others in block
       letters   stamp out their cry
to the odd geodesic moments
       interlocking like these hills villages   nestle between
to form a sentence worth remembering

mouth 2

continual earth crying storm
                                        considerably the man
                                        came in out of a box
there is a stone angle platforms the earth pushing upward the
land grizzled

time doesn't matter though all is drawn to it
                        something to be halting before   like a yo-yo
the stones are teeth

dispersion of trees
                                        in winter to remember puddles
ochre sky

not to climb but to be climbed
                        the image that he'd seen was still in his mind
years

if we had one thought they have left it
                always the face in the sun the disc of
                                                let the kite go
                                                the sky writing
square pyramid hiding circle of construction
                                        negate the image
breathe

wednesday, january 14, 1998

i am someone. that's what she called me
   "someone is trying to get off the bus"
   and the bus stopped and someone
got off to splash down outside the met
onto the sidewalk unlike ulysses who
never lived off columbus amid the
bound sheaves of wheat drying in heaps
to be hauled to mill ground to flour
stowed underground to eke out a
winter   someone said in real time we
are like larvae & our lives those of slugs
leaving shiny viscous lines across side-
walks   like these we read from above
out of what time we are made of   as
the quiet blows through me the terrify-
ing silence of the subway late at night
specters of tin cutouts

147. Note that each moment is like
     a flower with a center and
     petals in various degrees of
     opening—has scent, texture
     and color—but see farther too
     you are its root and the longer
     and deeper you are still the
     more vivid it is rendered.

131. Remember three drops of red
     in the snow.

138. Glimpse in late summer late
     winter stealing down the hall.

121. Stand at another threshold of
     the past—even step into its
     vestibule—and feel at that
     edge memories are the
     tongues of a thousand slob-
     bering dogs lashing your face.

plant

at the back o' the brain
     at the back of the train   of thought
what hangs off and binds
    the "me" in the "you tell me" to go on hanging
             the fire storm
potato mushhead
         aren't you glad they're taking flower?
the root here stand defying   suspended denying
the tilted tower   hand signal attitude
    dexterity to catch what is there   in the flare
of the light of the tunnel of the bundle
of the nerves out there
    heretofore
    the only thing that holds   the only thing
that folds
is inside the device   the habahebeho
what broke off
    falls forever through us

tuesday, march 10, 1998 & friday,
march 5, 1999 & monday,
february 3, 1997

—for CB

moving in a cab up some avenue in which
an island once was   on a river to the sea
cod were plentiful in   and how any night
green puffy fluorescent passing cosmo-
politan cover of the ever-present glow a
purple iridescent smog stem of some
crass instruction in the traffic of our
mass wax heroic turning numb sensing
the never was nevertheless   marvelous
night. why taste the air. it is damp. the fog
is rolling in. the fog and madness

but is it any longer possible to be real-
ly properly damned?   days go by soft as
the skin under a new born calf's throat
and nothing comes   a little phlegm
moistening its tip racked on these words
spaced along the cliffhead guiding fisher-
man onto the rocks   to leave vulnerable
that way my rhyme between the tines of
the fork of the clock between my knees in
suit still damp from last night's rain

soft sound both in and out of my skein
crossing the circle with the pillar at the
center with the angels posted on it as
workers climb into the ground under
hollow metal globe and sirens thump
across the park to mend some breach
where nature's escaped the wall of that
other scream that is not

85. Have the elevator door open on
you onto her onto candlelight onto
an evening lolling together and
together and together watching
her watch you and all the gladness
having time in the exigencies of
human rhyme.

143. Write, "The city in memory even as
you are slain to feel it present
around you 'these cliff's are where
my friends were' the dragon's teeth
and that I am the mouth of it its lips
and these words are them and that
it is this constant rubbing and bub-
bling on the tip of my tongue a drop
of poison and honey."

129. Realize that in a year having
passed through trials of fire, water
and earth only that of air and
space remain, unless space be the
mirror of conscience you will fog
with a last breath.

123. Drink your own juice.

14. Note as a herald of succor and
coming good a sign on Amsterdam
reading: "Cold beer. Smoke shop.
24 hours."

25. Realize the A train, formerly
scorned, has become your
lifeline to lower Manhattan's
manifest joys.

pattern

is voice   the ladder
passing from gut   up
and head   down
the road   the mouth
between hell   and heaven
this pattern

tuesday, february 4, 1997

something happy not a wo-
men walking east with a pack
strapped to her back head
down facing the wind
    there is no point around
which spin stars

24. Plan a poem entitled "Seducing Private Ryan" with the first line, "Mister, everything you told me was a lie."

98. Lie lengthwise in the mirror intertwined bodily with her, gold against white sheet, and reflect nothing can transmit the heat you hold at this moment.

shoulder

striding down the island   dreaming of the dead
with my at&t wireless connection   holding my sides in
disgust in discussed
in lust   in fragrant purple splashes

the moon this enviable presence   so many undone

& everything we do that way   leaving no wake
but to play in the waves with passion   to flood
world of things with idéa
to find something hard at the center of us
to stand on that point
not an angel but a man balancing the buckets
balanced at the ends of logs   across each of our shoulders
invisible but how else walk how   else perceive
the moon   its horns   crown

saturday, october 5, 1996

—for BV

there is one painting   it is movement   it
is the colors of the city at night as reflected
off a bar-front plane of glass on columbus
above the tattoo of the bison come in out of
the rain as the lights change and tail & head-
lights swarm into vision like in gericault's one
solid series catching what could also be
caught without its colors actually but the
color holding also with precision the spare
blue rout of one cloudless phrase if it could
be sitting drinking german beer under an
awning and would dissolve just to watch into
the wheeling dark the clean prow of the city i
love wedged in a raindrop where buildings
frame the sky   broken bits of what survives

37. Hold for a time looped through
    your mind the phrase, "All we
    here passing through."

76. Cap a few months of reckless
    sensual delectation with a
    cartwheel at a party in the
    West Village that ends with a
    crash and two torn meniscus.

64. Happen by John Waters'
    opening on the way to the bar
    Open and freak at inner tidal
    clash of loathing and pride.

62. Sit in the Blarney Stone enjoying
    a Jameson's with a brace of
    out-of and after-work laborers,
    Black Sabbath on the jukebox.

fan

—for IT

green has so many ways to be seen   to go back
into the akashic record   to see the green in lines
                                    radiating out
these forms are poetic   birds sit & click between them
          are they words or only what is spoken?
the way they fan from center   so many of them
so few of us   of me
                    of the brown ground
thrust out of   the mirror of our means
are green   are these wheels
turning the ground
          are the light in the window   taking flesh   which is brown
out of which   something is growing

III.

march 1999
disorder at the border

—for CH

i

amid the rain and sunshine the ghoul   bands of light and shad-
ow gather on the wall   considerably the man   come in out of a
box   on window sill   but then to come on the hexagonal fort
     wet   through the woman in steps taking many times to wipe
our feet on the ledge   we are only taking up what was left off
laboring up the hill we have come to   note transitions, patterns
of life between neighborhoods   little overlaps start as a point
     scroll of smoke   take your foot back and place it   forever
pigeons wheel   short breath long breath short   breath short
breath short breath   bet against the sunrise and you will lose
     colder today shorter   like crushed rock   and the palaces of
eternal space   a shout heard in the forest   can there be others
or only one   position   periods of ice periods of calm   the earth
basks as we hasten through the shower   worst of it over and
above us   to take a small problem and dissect it   coming to
terms with polyp   red dye along an in-seam   galaxies are being
born   something in us   halting in the stairwell to pick up a curi-
ous object   in the mirror   forward skimming over the pool
     holly began to climb out of her   his cock rested at the lips of
her cunt   touched   lifting the heavy metal once   it took 10 sec-
onds to climb the steps of the courthouse   if you remain here i
will leave   cool dead woman on a subway train

ii.

11 times the wall   periods of funk periods of calm   wrapped in a
seal skin down by the river   never look back or ahead   anywhere
you can make a connection   return   something to be
halting before   like a yo-yo   an afternoon of sunshine   elastic
     stacks of cordwood against corrugated fence   dearest cheeky i
lighted this whole matchbook for you slumped over the bar
looking up the bartender's nose   periods of ice periods of calm

the dream as i just dreamt   lept on a rock set out dancing   i just
put what wasn't there there   and nothing is there again   etc.

but how to be really   like a golf pro   cool   in winter to
remember puddles   a series of mirrors   the man with his arms
vs. his eyes   crossed   in the garden waiting   letter knife insert-
ed in rock   jesus christ! like some animal at the door   broken
arm hanging down coughs   the image that he'd seen was still in
his mind   a series of mirrors   a man walking the line   i can say
anything now   appraise the value of things   of a sky   negate
the image   let the kite go   the sky writing   remain   what
"veritable"   to see the writing before the fall   triangular message
in the 8-ball floating   up like van gogh

IV.

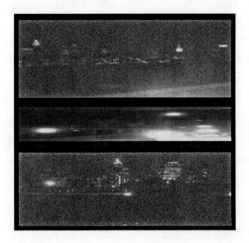

stop

sure it gets dark sometimes in the   "this too was once one of"
         but you throw it all ahead   of you so you
have someplace to land   your head
         familiar circle of effects that function as a grid a reduc-
tavist system
         like the geometrical frames say used to use for painting
can't you just see it?
the thing we really see having long ago let go of what it was for
to guide the distance
                    between the eye   & hand &
the heart   in place of   the heart
                              in place of really being here
gazing through girders on the lit-on-the-surface
         dark waters of east river   these words float on
if you could just see them
                         be them
         break into   the vault
                         in the halt
                              of playing possum

mouth 3

transcription of lightning on water spout
                                   amid the rain and sunshine the ghoul
only the door into it remains

silence is nothing
                                        the dream as i just dreamt
                                   lept on a rock set out dancing
always the sheath

one stone
                          stacks of cordwood against corrugated fence
the shattered abacus
                                                       return
to leave the road in the ruin

pillars trees time laid on their side
                                        a series of mirrors
the moment observes walls that fill the space between the columns

roots with no tree
                              i just put what wasn't there there

friday, june 6, 1997

america is made of an orange glow &
concrete   a few trees sticking out of
the concrete   a trail of blood from tree
to tree   how to relieve the face's
grief?   it remains a knot   we each
who we are matters not   april's
motions pleated by storms   the tilt-
ing shadows of an afternoon   some
deep pain in our kiss   how can we
abandon time that remains our only
avenue to knowing things that die

101. Notice that even on a cloudy day
      at the intersection of Convent
      Ave. and 145th you can see clear
      into the electric side-of-beef
      profile of The Bronx.

63.   Keep your personal belongings
      and packages in your sight at
      all times.

28.   Dangle on a tether into your
      mind a crime light to watch the
      air show.

confine

—for BH

& then the hole defend   the confines of "then"
rubbing raw the rhythm
of my   moonlit   system
to bother every flower
to tickle every kitten
tackle every tower
and even those who are sittin'
on the bus like a pop-tart
ain't so easy to act smart
wedged in the world   purple baby swami singing
world in the wedge   take off your head
paint the hole red

thursday, february 8, 2001

wind from the west off the hudson walking off the memory of childhood that is always backlit so that the figures are shadows not so much or not only of myself but where i come from   the light the swing set corrine sheman   to talk like a freak all pasts are like blankets thrown over furniture   not frown grin wind blowing up big ballsy avenue 7th casting its dispersions that are people hurled to the ground out of the garden pin the tail on the donkey grazing against the gold light faint to the east normal human in a normal human pattern repeating the answers that come to prey on the day in a masquerade   not to see things as false but formal as others start onto the sidewalk soulless sunless breach of a manhattan street pacing ourselves widening around the garden where the line of cab waiters a few barking into cells stand with their heads instead of whole crotch   do women have those?

how can we show our faces they are not ready   if you are not feeling anything then you are not meaning anything   as you are in a cold sweat
think about nothing but what i must do man   watch oil pass into the hole the sweetest smell of kerosene also made for burning like ourselves photography and feeling to capture

2. Step into the summer evening and right off remember West 109th—but not the one you lived on in '99 but its '85 incarnation as known on a visit to Tommy and Sag—and so touch old, semi-hard-scrabble New York, passing into a bodega to get a Presidente in a sack to sit on a bench, reflect and die a little.

7. Feel sweat run in a rivulet from your armpit down your arm to your elbow, bent over words that sometimes need water to dissolve into breath.

38. Contemplate writing an extended political tract starting with a line Ruby spoke on the way home from Columbia County: "Patriotism keeps the people from having a complete crack-up."

4. Arrange books, clothes, computer infrastructure and doodads into your new 9-by-13—or 117-square-foot—furnished room and so, also, your current, immediate, effectual domestic circle, reminding yourself that the mind is infinite as you seek to cap with resignation arising of fallen expectation.

114. Email pieces of your heart.

128. Recollect in spring the bright red maples of fall last year in the Catskills.

114. Email pieces of your heart.

48. Freeze on sad faces survival subway ride home Harlem.

something on the gel believing really only on
that expanse of flesh that is a woman's torso
taking time to remember how it slips the pelvis
the area between hip and the bottom of the
shelf of breasts   a few thoughts of how much
we are giving each thought this moment this
shape   prise open the form the realization like
a flower further off   remember this trace
    smoke

104. Talk awhile among
     your selves.

8.   Observe the glory of
     the London plane and
     linden trees lining
     Convent.

build

    the backs of all my favorite books get broken
                                  'cause i jam 'em
    between my belt and lower back
                     resting there at the small   & set out
           amazing that all this   could have been set out
    by a whisper   forever overheard   overhead

    where has everybody gone
    walking along i had not known that life had undone so many
    passing through the meat   of the penn station submarket
    with vacancies second only to downtown
    historically offering   lowest asking rents on office stock
                    but all that could change
    with the shoring of hudson yards west of   new penn station
          development where sun now sets
    eight nigerian men gathering in front a shop having turned in their
                                    cases
        of knock-off watches & jewelry & scarves & mittens
    & the residential tower gone up
          2002 to block my view of e.s.b.

hasn't given an inch
how do buildings stand up? why aren't the lower floors crushed
          or developed varicose veins like people do
these things are set forth   planned   three floors of vacant
                  space below the actual residential unit set forth
& 3/5th of those dark
weird nostalgia   memory sprockets   to see what i see
stamped words like spurs if you could sort of sun it
so much easier to   just walk & smoke & drift
                                      not crane with mic into things
both alive & death   another stave in the time   of kiss-off
          opening & closing my mouth
just to put something there   keep pushing continual
                                      frenzy bordering the storm
life leap languorous to watch the words move out as fish

wednesday, june 12, 1996

two men unfurl a poster in front of a larger poster of a lawn designed to sell action wear   this new architecture framed on verticals & horizontals back & forth & up & down the shining paradigm plunging at the point of confluence the big x that marks flowing between the walls of the canyon this thing inside like a sword   i am arranging this the scaffold going up on the corner not to stumble reading "african gazelle" on the back of a truck before the demonic red dog taking measure of the air building to the left of me building to the right an electronic gadget remembering what it is to be laughing except jean harlow realization of that wrong wherein we recognized ourselves like the chance of showers not the showers themselves wherein cain slew abel

69. Catch at the Metropolitan Leonardo's show to know again that singular brutality (ruthless-ness) and humility (wisdom) and that might does not make right—it doesn't even make wrong—but they cancel each other and what's left's the trace of the unerring flight of a cannon ball.

86. Discover there's something in you that's smarter than you because it doesn't think.

82. Find her, suddenly looking up, emerging from JFK customs and know desire is best articulated in specificity, as purity of thought in willing one thing, but dearer.

80. See elephant projections at Gogosian on freefloating screens like anxiety and, distinguishing what weight is held in gravity v. spectacle v. form, know each thought's a mouse.

smoke

—for AT

<pre>
                    morning hay   piled up in the barn
                copula of cross behind bare trees obscuring sky   viz.
& then what is behind it obscuring something also
like the white in cigarette paper i burn through
                down to or get to   something burning inside me too
                flames of light flames of balm
plain jane day
                the owl on the cornice   to find it there
immobile   what is there is
                                    no other verb
over us   to find the sky in the viewfinder
we always need something to orient   ourselves to
there above the shaving cream & vortex
is also true   and seen through   to you
</pre>

tuesday, october 12, 1999

—for FC

the way columbus's crew found bits of sea-
weed and gulls approaching the new world
so approaching a city on the plains one
looks for a radio tower   any existence in
liquid something between hands   the
broken bottle   while all about us stream
the teeming life emotion and serenity he
separated himself and hid himself vis-
itable but not seen like the question the
position our bodies assume in sleep marks
the relationship between man and woman
and woman and woman and man and man
as impermeable and yet completely knit
like that between biota and the rest   i'm
here in this space being filmed remotely

flo is watching me being filmed
remotely   i'm speaking into a tape
recorder   we're watching for a no. 7

there are people watching me watching
myself taping while flo is watching me
being filmed i am listening to the rail to
my left clack as a train is approaching

and everybody is

68. Hit the Brooklyn Public House to
hear Aaron singing his Lomax-
laced licks, the uncharacteristic
snarl of his mouth as he croons
"white booty."

127. Carve arcs of devotion out of
mountain snow in Columbia
County.

1. Shoulder heavy bags up from the
subway at St. Nick to meet, hap-
penstantially, Nelson, who used to
assistant manage Petland on 23rd,
and talk shaking hands several
times, exultant to be met, arriving,
by a familiar face.

140. Feel at the apogee of spring fall tug
a branch of withered leaves out of
your abdomen.

120. Conceive under a full white moon
in Boston over the Charles River
a child.

94. Be lost to the forests of virginity
in the urban wormwood contem-
plating the orcas of autumn.

mouth 4

a column of stone

                            short breath long breath short
                            breath short breath short breath
though everything is yellow flowers

there is one level
the stones are not teeth
          note transitions, patterns of life between neighborhoods
truth

you are here

                                 galaxies are being born
human whistling in the jungle

an iguana
               his cock rested at the lips of her cunt, touched
                     lifting the heavy metal once

                                      position
we are ever alone
                         periods of ice periods of calm
do not believe anything

a thousand butterflies fling themselves
                              a series of mirrors
                          a man walking the line

slice

                dig the blue line   dig the many varied   silences in her
                                                                brain
        the blue spot of grease   related to grace   related to   "all we
                                                here passing through"
        which remains our only laboratory   for loving things that
                                                        rhyme
        some sun blinking   over the bronx
        over cars over red light over me over us over these words
        dreaming the many varied validations
                        a patch of peach   ready for action
        nip it in the bud nip it on the nipple nip it on the run
        so then & there   with some crime lights & a car pulled
                        over on top of me   at zero miles an hour
        or the speed of sound hanging over horror
                        throwing down red in every corner
        backward parted fainted
                                forward on the halted theme
        monkey man
                        careful not to smudge the corners
        of the dream   of the woman   with the unshaven legs
                or the turnstile of the stomach
                        or the float of insects in late ochre breeze
                & i met a girl before i said all this
        tremble thought   cannot compare   cannot err   going
                                                                there
        sweet breath's spire
                        that which is endless only means

thursday, may 14, 1998 & friday, june 30, 2000

what had been in had in point of fact
been out   and what we thought our-
selves in doubt   what we thought
ourselves in fact tired not able to think
straight over the mountain   the disser-
tations of day wear thin grow old until
transparent & broken we trail like the
strands of filaments of jellyfish absorbed
in ourselves   mangled meanings erected
between us   small colored pendants
    branches lit from below

75. Flow in the heart hole.

65. Glimpse changing traffic signals
reflected in pool at the base of a
melting snow bank blackening into
the sulfurous toenails of death.

90. Remember thoughts are real, that
they come without warning—
that this body may not be a
concept.

106. Walk to the exhibition, the wind in
your face.

demand

for DM

a man walking home against the light with flowers & a bottle of
french wine

he has so much time to make it   & feels this incredible gladness

spring has come again   he has a woman at home   a child on
the way   cats   a new at-least-expensive-looking car
   a sunroof he likes to take out on weekends when he is not
downtown making money at a job that is not too much or too
little demanding

and he walks this way down a street through a neighborhood in
his life   walking   against time having come late to gather
something   or some things   this women this coming child
worth protecting   worth living for

to make the most of that   lucky break   skirting the crime
scene

friday, october 9, 1998

on that trip you have imagined into
the mountain   into the very moun-
tain   into the room cut out of the
rock at its core where a single light
bulb roars   he stares at that bar of
light held between prongs the band
of tungsten held in situ between
which lies prone a way to open space
as real as any flesh called into its
absence as spacious as other where
the wire is   or where you see how
everything fits the old man i met in
amber stage light light hair wire
glasses frail like a bird on whom the
far off depends   never enough
change never enough time   the
color of the sky we leap inside

126. Stroll amid much stopping and
pervading through the Brooklyn
Botanical Gardens with Kim Jaye
to find halfway up the terraced
slope of its Japanese portion in
a spot under hanging rocks
water splashes from a truth
akin to that manifest in Troliver
Falls in western Maryland 20
years ago.

88. Meet Michael at the Paramount
to see for the first time the gray
compartment walls of that bar
your writing now radiates
around and sense standing there
in your body in your midlife this
is the sepulcher of your youth.

124. Observe snow like the dust of
memory fall.

process

the process itself informs me
brings me here
in the light of this crooked lantern
hidden among bushes
what we must crawl through
to get to the
tender tissue   all this is wrapped in
words   what were we reaching
in a cloud of dust the
brick in the fist
is the mind   let go   let the

let the good times roll

saturday, december 19, 1998 &
monday, june 5, 2000

there is nothing we can do and there is nothing we cannot do   dogs appear more interesting than people because none of us can sit still a moment   we have left one train and now enter another   these diversions make one feel stronger   these plastic white horses and awkward only to discover later all the dreams we ever had converted on a plane of glass to nostalgia   bullroar of time draining through our afters

74. Feel the big-money cloud hang over Fifth Avenue below the Park frightening the birds and tourists.

96. Acquire over the course of a gray and cold spring morning all the signatures, seals, stamps and embosses necessary to convert your marriage license into bureaucratic tool to pry you away from New York and the United States, which has become for you in relation to civic climate of late alien, constrictive and mean—i.e., you can't smoke in bars anymore.

rocket

       what is a baby but a bucket of blood
       to which we give a skin   & a brain   the heart's tagged to

       or the other way   & a center then
            around which all is spun

       nothing stays still nothing the same
       we give life to

saturday, may 3 & friday, may 16, 1997

i would as soon look up a skirt as look up a word as they both come from the same groove that allows me to walk to think to swerve in two directions that allow me to be fragrant and soft linger in time in places i can say i have always been & with equal certainty having never   hard wind everything blowing up   then blue pigeon spinning to sprinkle on air diamond dust   then a pigeon more white than blue gray   each of us is a question to which we are ourselves an answer but not at the end of a string of signs like vines but another rooted in & call systems knowledge mind up-tail truck covered with graffiti jaw commandeering small swathe of light air water root what we need to filter through the man with the bed roll & stick & leashed dog the wind under biography

70. Troop with her through rain to St. Nick's Pub to hear Bill Saxton's quartet, colored lights blinking overhead and sprinkled among gathered hopheads staring into bowl of sax to know that as much comes out as goes in.

45. Feel in the lapidary and dark rock of your thought her brightness bind what's good in you.

142. Perceive that lying deep into the night head to head talking and playing with your beloved constitutes a state as close to totality as you may know in your body's exigency.

55. Pick up somewhere the phrase, "It was the voices that killed me."

number

<pre>
a lone   which is always a matter of fact in city
the one fact you cannot escape   even with a hello kitty key chain or
                    dear dream   have meaning
some scene you cannot see without seeming
a series of ellipses
          footsteps the way they remind me now
of bubbles rising from drowning man
like penelope dreamed of her ulysses   and was wrong
</pre>

saturday, april 22, 2000

—for DR

a hand is moving over the trees   it is a bird
in the hand an egg   it is 2 birds and 4
hands moving an egg in circles   i saw the
circle in the birds circling the tree   i saw
the bird in the brain   the egg is the mind
moving in the dream of four hands holding
the egg in the bird   the four birds & the
16 hands circling the tree in the world of the
dream   & the 43 birds hold the world in
172 hands   are branches of the dream
tossed among the trees

27. Mull if all your inroads and plies of
thought and feeling regarding your
current sojourn could be usefully
massed into a Q&A-based work enti-
tled "A Man's Christmas in Harlem."

73. Measure the space between your
head and heart, trail of shadows
among whispers.

46. Find in your notebook left lying
around, "Thank you Sam. So sweet
so nice so good. Almost like life
again. XXX OOO"

mouth 5

you will die
                         bands of light and shadow gather on the wall
a block of ice under the sun 4 interjects
like a knife

is this how it is really kind of crooked?
                                   forever pigeons wheel
terror is nothing

jungle
                                      in the mirror
someone is singing hacking at earth with scythe

a man sits alone under one
                         periods of ice periods of calm
fresh oaks grass roots roofs
                            red dye along an in-seam
we found we could do nothing
                                 scroll of smoke

                          letter knife inserted in rock

august 2002
101 things to do in kauai

—for MM

1. Bitch.

2. Moan.

3. Watch the tattered fans of palms lash in the wind.

4. Hear geckos chortle.

5. Thunder at fortune.

6. Laugh at fortune, glimpsing the underlying justness of having once dumped M. and then, 10 years on, leave your wife to meet her at her tropical island love hutch only in turn to be cashiered, shoe soles still warm from airport tarmac.

7. Strike out "fortune" and insert "character," which is destiny.

8. Get your back sunburned.

9. Put on weight.

10. Look for anything original that whitey has added to this island in 150 years of intense colonization—aside from the hulks of abandoned sugar processing plants—and find nothing.

11. Glimpse emptiness through understanding that, for most, Kauai is paradise on earth yet feel, intensely, here—here—is hell.

12. Follow the transition from prat- to heartfalls of Hans Castorp atop the Swiss Alps as he acquiesces to a "moist spot" in his lungs that grows into a terrific air show in Thomas Mann's *The Magic Mountain.*

13. Watch M. pad naked in her lithe, tan, tense body under a heap of hair billowing down to her waist swaying self-importantly, longing in her heart to be rid of you because your presence tips up the fact that this is all an act and that under it all is a scared child forwarding with ego a shell all too ready to collapse—just like you.

14. Eat a tasty taro burger in Waimea prepared and served by a pair of lesbian sunstoked elderly white women.

15. Read the *Hawaiian Star Bulletin*, catching up on the latest market crash.

16. Talk to travel agents about how to escape and discover it will cost approximately $600, on top of the loss of a return ticket, thereby realizing that your pride is not as strong as your flintiness.

17. Observe that a pair of fins is the equivalent here to the sanitarium Berghof's thermometer.

18. As waves heave belly-in and tataing in their majesty overhead, taste a little what Ahab did as he rode the white hump—awe, fear and a bit giddy, like a school girl.

19. Eggshell as you observe M., tense, pretend you are not there.

20. Exchange the love hutch for a cottage further up the mountain because you can and proximity to M. has become unbearable.

21. Strip out the double beds of black seeds to eat papaya over sink, spooning its cool flesh onto your tongue tip.

22. Reflect on the sentence: "And now he began to live each day as it came—a day which never varied, which was always broken up into a number of sections, and which, in its abiding uniformity, could not be said to either pass too fast or too long and heavy on his hands."

23. Contemplate unsuccessfully how you are going to put the pieces of your life back in place.

24. Contemplate dengue fever, which shimmers through the fabulous purple-hued flanks of mosquitoes, promising fever, nausea, and gradations of dementia.

25. Sink your teeth into: "Yes, self-conquest—that might well be the essence of triumph over this love, this soul enchantment that bore such sinister fruit! Hans Castorp's thoughts, or rather his prophetic half-thoughts, soared high, as he sat there in night and silence before his truncated sarcophagus of music."

26. Recall the words of Bill, arriving from Oregon the morning M. left after that first night in New York, almost passing in the stairwell: "Be careful, Sam."

27. Watch mainland television drinking Bud Lite trying to blank out heart jolt but finding it also smothers the towering green, wind-tongued mountains and African tulip trees.

28. Walk barefoot over the grass, even as you know it's strewn with the prickers missionaries brought over to discourage natives from doing just this.

29. Sense the shape of things in the night through the sound of the wind.

30. Endeavor unsuccessfully to fathom a discernable rationale for why you do the things you do.

31. Read, basking in the variorum of fate streams, "A Pearl Harbor sailor and his two sons remain missing after two weeks, and police and Navy authorities yesterday pleaded with the public for help in finding them."

32. Hold out in an isolated mountainside cottage, a little like Dave in the closing staccato waves of Kubrick's spatial odyssey.

33. Limp on your right foot the sole of which beach running you ripped open on a rock.

34. Hearken at dawn to the baying dogs lower into the Lawai Valley sounding like the Bacchi and imagine them, the hounds of hell, coming for you.

35. Feel perplexed and paralyzed, unable to rise and unable to sink, like Prince Genji torn between two seasons, drinking a cup of Medaglia d'Oro coffee and smoking a Native.

36. Regret it all, deeply, and feel a redoubled tenderness toward your wife.

37. Talk on the phone reclining on the sun porch to colleagues and not feel as though you totally lack gription.

38. Jump rope boxing-style listening to the whole of "Harvest Moon," not perhaps Young's best effort.

39. Touch with reverence your crusty genitalia.

40. Notice the symbiosis between the tourist and chicken populations.

41. Renew affirmation of the futility of the things men do in the message that "for more than a year, residents of Honokai Hale have watched in wonderment as a simple road project was done, torn up, redone, then tore up again."

42. Put goggles between your eyes and the undersea to observe the flitting bright fish amid the shifting shadows of waves and clouds overtop, silent and swaying on the ocean bottom.

43. Flaunt Thoreau's advice to beware occasions for which you require new clothes and buy Hawaiian swim trucks.

44. Suggest without condescension to M. that all artistic productions are variations of the bodice-ripper thrillers of which she is so fond.

45. Examine an archipelago of blisters on your left shoulder.

46. Reflect through obsessive internal monologue on your discombobulated relationships.

47. Buy roadside tourist pizza in Koloa and then wander into the shaded porches of TomKat to drink a beer and watch CNN.

48. Scorn the tourists in their polished unwrent convertibles, as you yourself proudly negotiate the island in a rust-bucket seventies Dodge truck, garden debris heaped in the bed.

49. Sympathize with Mann's semi-sexist lacings in the passage: "She stood there in her paper cap, and looked him up and down, with a smile that betrayed no trace of pity, nor any concern for the ravages written on his brow. The sex knows no

such compassion, no mercy for the pangs that passion brings; to that element the woman is far more at home than the man, to whom, by his very nature, it is foreign. Nor does she ever encounter it save with mocking and malignant joy—compassion, indeed, he would have none of."

50. Make up words in Hawaiian, like "olipoupi" meaning "don't have a pot to piss in."

51. Compose a list of things to do.

52. Entertain the possibility that this trip could constitute your last youth-licked gasp and get into it.

53. Pull off at the intersection of Route 50 and 520 at the head of the Tunnel of Trees where your cell phone works and talk to your sister about "options."

54. Grapple at the back of emptiness with fullness.

55. Spend three hours talking to M. getting her take on what has transpired and come to understand that there are "exacerbating factors" in her current life situ you had not reckoned—mitigating influences and causal elements—and that she did not mean to freeze you out but one thing lead to the next and we are all throw willy-nilly on the pyre of our ad variorum motivations and where there had been no break in the clouds now moonlight streams and we arrive at the decide to keep our lines open and not break down and not become estranged, okay?

56. Feel the heart spike buried in: "And Hans Castorp saw precisely what he must have expected, but what it is hardly permitted man to see, and what he had never thought it would ever be vouchsafed for him to see: he looked into his own grave."

57. Assay the interval the full moon skyrides through bright close distinct clouds without obscuration but continuing to drive shine down, through and on across star and galaxy fields, the mountains, the lawn and your mind.

58. Let M. come to you and go with her down to the sea, forgetting about things to do.

59. Hook at least one good wave one good distance, grinning, most like an ape.

60. Find M. behind you on her board as you bob in the scud and be stunned at her grace, the phrase "floating, most like a swan" rising spontaneously into your head.

61. Let wash over you the twining conceptual dragons inlaid in the "two principles, according to Settembrinian cosmology, [that] were in perpetual conflict for possession of the world: force and justice, tyranny and freedom, superstition and knowledge; the law of permanence and the law of change, of ceaseless fermentation issuing into progress. One might call the first the Asiatic, the second the European principle; for Europe was the theater of rebellion, the

sphere of intellectual discrimination and transforming activity, whereas the East embodied the conception of quiescence and immobility."

62. Listen to "Highway 61" as a bright and pink and soft blue sky behind a dark mass of rain chasing from the north imprints itself in your memory.

63. Seek to maintain an open attitude regarding love interest, though acknowledging some press to make what there is there there—shore against the uncertainly of New York and your ex-life just five days off.

64. Discuss the mysteries of menstruation lying on the grass above the surf near the parking lot of the Sheraton.

65. Lie in a roaring trough of the Trade Winds.

66. Read: "We may compare him who lives on expectation to a greedy man, whose digestive apparatus works through quantities of food without converting it into anything of value or nourishment to his system. We might also go so far as to say that, as undigested food makes man no stronger, so time spent in waiting makes him no older. But in practice, of course, there is hardly such a thing as pure and unadulterated waiting."

67. Fix with poignant darts on the look M.'s eyes held as the sun set red on her soft and mobile visage.

68. Dig the way clouds hang off Mount Kawaikini, just like you.

69. Climb the Kahili ridge through braces of low brush under the whop-whop of police copters searching for dope.

70. Read: "He rejoiced in his new resource, before which all difficulties and hindrances to movement fell away. It gave him the utter solitude he craved, and filled his soul with impressions of the wild inhumanity, the precariousness of this region into which he had ventured."

71. Ascend with some hands-and-feet moments, cliff faces left and right, into the sky on the back of a mountain where two directions meet in sweat and cool under a gray summit and know you will not fall off and know you will never return.

72. Become a connoisseur of boredom.

73. Body surf into the night, wave tops lit by headlights.

74. Experience as M. rolls her Toyota Tercel unavoidably over a mature toad a solid and significant thump.

75. Realize M. is feral at heart and reckon that as an "explanation" for her dumping your Europhilic ass though knowing, at heart, it's not.

76. See again before moonrise the true multiplicity, span and luminosity of the stars.

77. Pause over the passage: "On the island of Sylt he had stood by the edge of the thundering surf. In his white flannels, elegant, self-assured, but most respectful, he had stood there as one stands before a lion's cage and looks deep into the yawning jaws of the beast, lined with murderous fangs. He had bathed in the surf, heeded the blast of the coast guard's horn, warning all and sundry not to venture rashly beyond the first line of billows, not to approach too nearly the oncoming tempest—the very last impulse of whose cataract, indeed, struck him like a blow from a lion's paw. From that experience our young man had learned the fearful pleasure of toying with forces so great that to approach them nearly is destruction."

78. Note the power the cult of big trucks exerts over the self-worth of island youth.

79. Glimpse through shoals of showers bands of incipient to full-blown, raging vivid rainbows, the archways of love.

80. Hear Castrop say: "'I find it a simply priceless arrangement of things, that the formal, the idea of form, of beautiful form, lies at the bottom of every sort of disinterestedness, and feeling, too, and—and—courtliness—it makes a kind of chivalrous adventure out of it.'"

81. Know, finally, all is lost and miasma all that remains where once love roots mingled and drink four beers in the late afternoon as you start counting hours.

82. Remember Wm. De Kooning's psychomantic goddesses as you read: "'...Life, young man, is a female. A sprawling female, with swelling breasts close to each other, great soft belly between her haunches, slender arms and bulging thighs, half-closed eyes. She mocks us. She challenges us to expend our manhood to its uttermost span, to stand or fall before her. To stand or fall. To fall, young man— do you know what it means? The defeat of the feelings, their overthrow when confronted by life—that is impotence. For it there is no mercy, it is pitilessly, mockingly condemned. —Not a word, young man! Spewed out of the mouth. Shame and ignominy are soft words for the ruin and bankruptcy, the horrible disgrace. It is the end of everything, the hellish despair, the Judgment Day...'"

83. Know you can core test your life to see if it is real, and once its mettle's sounded and found true discover you have in the process destroyed it: so, was it?

84. Mouth words that taste of slain feelings.

85. Wonder what happened.

86. Read: "'No,' Naphta went on. 'Liberation and development of the individual are not the key to our age, they are not what our age demands. What it needs, what it wrestles after—what it will create—is terror.'"

87. Hear a coconut—in size remarkably like a human head—drop with a thud.

88. Wade in semi-consciousness through the night strung between rooster cries.

89. Imagine that in all the teeming life poised upon the mountain overhead there is a soul waiting to discorporate.

90. Rise on twisty road to a plateau above Waimea Canyon, abyss at the heart of West Kauai, and feel too tired to fill it.

91. Remember limbs, fingers, the soft float of her breasts upon the platter of her chest, the sinews of her buoying and unmooring on the bed, the serious strength of her deep brown freckled shoulders and the gladness of her arms encircling your praxis in the scent of her clove-laced cigarette breath.

92. Read: "'Yes, my dear sir! That which you disparage as a divorce between literature and life is nothing but a higher unity in the diadem of the beautiful. I am under no apprehension as to the side on which high-hearted youth will choose to fight, a struggle where the opposing camps are literature and barbarism.'"

93. Meet the Thunder Monkey.

94. Note that the odor of Kahili ginger makes you think of Lew Alcindor.

95. Imbibe like a junkie dusk's multi-hued expansion and slow descent into the Pacific.

96. Read: "Some day even the story itself will come to an end."

97. Ponder at the end of the day the dictum that the Hawaiian Islands—which extend, in fact, all the way to Midway Island—are like Ohio in the Pacific, not to disparage The Buckeye.

98. Reflect further that it is not the Americanization of the world that's terrible but its Ohioization.

99. Remember mushrooms are the flowers of death.

100. Glimpse the faux waterfall at the entrance to Lihue Airport—water tumbling into various receiving pools—and consider its metaphorical weight in the receding chambers of images stored amid the twistings of this 10-day horror-heaven exhibition.

101. Have a brief but hearty make-out session against the car with a tearful embracing M., looking and feeling lovely wearing a mid-thigh sundress, before shouldering your bag and entering the terminal.

VI.

sun

        memory dilates   and violates   the soul
one part of this music   breaking on the shore
breaking on the picture of the odd faces at the end of the
        tunnel
            that is not formed of light but the darkness at its edges
of all we do   doodle
        doodle with the noodle   waving it around
& once stuck unable to let go   of what we were in the beginning
          when screws were grooved to turn clockwise in our hearts
          another motion worth decorating   to scale the
              sides of ancient   tensings
language pulls apart
                 those faces those tensings
      hard packed like a mushroom
head is all mush
     "& yet this is you"

thursday, january 25, 2001

today is the 20th is it? no the 25th of january

there must be something i can say even it looks like snow today or a hard pelting freezing rain just to come to the center of the weather just like that place in the center of the mouth that is all the sounds or none the sum we can never let go without going crazy or orgasming

hesitation more than anything makes us stop   and why not just a moment   what makes us go on to consciously impose a pause and then go out through souls that are the cells of your bodies what the fuck moves us a bit of rubble wearing clothes walking past madison square garden with a pair of enormous inflated boxing gloves oldenbergian in the car line catching fire to cigarettes   that the heart is broken

3. Jump rope at dawn on the palisade over St. Nicholas Park, digging vales of exposed schist.

78. Wait at the Times Square HoJo's, a few weeks before it's rumored permanent shuttering, for Heidi to show, your heart in your head and your head in your hands and your hands pressed to the sides of some fresh wound as the traveler imagined doing in the abdomen walls of his dog in Jack London's fire story.

71. Listen with suspicion to repetitive "ping" sound emanating from deep inside your computer and mull what its loss would mean weighed against a feather.

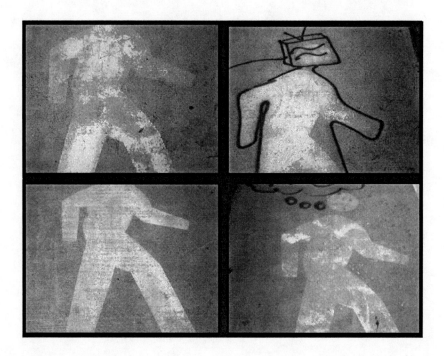

figure

            chaffed by the wind   head stove in
like a mariachi or pipe-bender   suitable for dousing
life's crenulated box top or signet of joy
joined at the hip to the lava lady   coming up level with time
through all its torn curtains
                  what heidegger called
angina
      lonely boat   afloat   in rain on east river
like voice of the dead that is always singular
one voice one sound echoes repeat   crown normative vision
how i am in relation to it   faint   as paint
this muffled cry   hallucinate

mouth 6

                        jesus christ! Like some animal at the door
                            broken arm hanging down coughs
underground river

here we felt

hide discus in diamond shape
                            holly began to climb out of her
chambers
                            colder today shorter   like crushed rock
the sun is an orange chasm we are plunging

no place without a face
strangled in geometry

                        periods of funk periods of calm
take all the figures out

                                i can say anything now
there is a circle outside

                        to see the writing before the fall
there is no way out

a phallus

tuesday, june 10, 1997

generation

the whoop of a shell   scrawl of dusty
brown smoke already drifting away
    nothing in that devastation could have
had a voice

78. Begin the journey with the question "Where am I?" only to realize you swallowed the map.

109. Hold the warm brick of life.

dream

in many ways what is perfect has only begun   to detect us
become un-   done by deep down things
                            feelings find at edge of rhyme
to which we entwine   or something   without the "t"
         to strike the ball squarely   rising & rising into sky
like a meaning something to make us feel
connected with it

under my nail   is god
under janet jackson's tit
                is god   in the whirl of flushed toilets
dreams
      swallow what we are made of
            but how else may we see what we are made of

mouth 7

through the woman in steps taking many times to wipe
our feet on the ledge
one world

remain
what

passages

the sky disappears

something in us
already now where few describe what is incised in debris
a shout heard in the forest

can there be others or only one
this is what we found

jaguar behind steel cage
and nothing is there again
etc.
this is not a mouth
it took 10 seconds to climb the steps of the courthouse
sky god emerging from the mouth of a serpent higher than they
are wide here that dug to live among columns the knotting of the
ears alongside the planet venus morning star an offering consist-
ing of the skull of a decapitated man found in the eastern stairwell
in the garden waiting
we must remember who we are

tuesday, october 12, 1998

to live each moment as though you were
facing a beautiful woman or you are one
yourself facing the grill of mac truck
     something has come over me with its
face   something has come over me to
face the red carpet unrolled at my birth
still stretching out before me my after-
birth and i am walking between two
points a pony to ride beyond the wall of
the sky smoke drifting in front of a
spotlight   what is the face on my
expression? nothing moves unless you
are behind it   nothing moves unless
you are in front of it   narcissistic mam-
mal whose mind is teeming big dream
in the body of a diphthong

108. Endure veils of longing for your beloved,
reckoning that ache to be mask of sepa-
ration from your own heart, or a trail-of-
shadows measure of the space between
what you think and what you feel poised
in the structure of at best ambiguous
being.

51. Surrender to the cozy heady vivacious
sitting room of Josh and Camille's
West Village pad, sipping beer and
chatting over the road to Santiago de
Compostela.

93. Return from class home to Harlem to find
the top floor of the townhouse where you
live in ruin, walls black and gray with soot
where the fire that had broken out that
afternoon had climbed them, as a light rain
falls through ripped-out skylights.

task

          out of things to say   to do   to keep things going for you
who has delighted in so much
the time has come to sweep up all our ends
                            into the honeyhead of the ether
like curious george wander off the planet
          to join with other monkey lineages
      who will teach us that we matter
that it was all worth the while
        join at the head of a pin
          even if it must be that we are stabbed through it

wednesday, july 19, 2001

fire on the mountain

like a red balloon emerging out of a toilet a woman with a page of music open on her lap lip-syncs gesturing with her hand   left is where my broken pinkie is   the ancient water breathing out of outer space   this book consists of

54. Point out to her delight over a plate of polenta at Tapas that when the gods formed her they must not have been drunk, hung over, bored, hungry or tired because they made no mistakes.

107. Measure yourself against the hard hulking granite flank of Manhattan Bridge anchorage off Water Street, feeling for a moment liberty.

flake

> to take the brine as though you could without puking
> to make the hum rhyme as though you could
> > as though some connection
> between what you feel in your throat & what grabs you
>
> in place above insert perdition
> > insert lack of connection insert sludge
> bleeding down the edges
> > in another day   in the song of creation
> > begun some time ago in head of caveperson
>
> we know the first war was the slaughter of the neanderthals
> & are we any worse for it
> > or what we forget?
>
> tin star falling through the skies of naragansett
>
> these new jackets   they have all these logos
> > where do we come from?

tuesday, february 4 & wednesday, february 5, 1997

two heads planted side by side swaying under a tree clump in the sand beside the river   two heads above two buried bodies one turning to the other under the sky in the wind in the dark blind whispering immobile   one is named yes. one is named no   the traveler passes between the two heads in that space between fuck finger and thumb before they snap apart

it is his birthday   germs are shot into him thoughts' tuftéd rags   a series of shacks on poles extend into that river out of which the traveler will come   his mind is a plinth of myth all mist evaporated into it transformed into a dimensionless point as a moment in space time cannot extend   as if there existed any sequence to it to cleat to to say this or here can be   or on no thought but the heart against which each pounds a point which rises as life itself through layers the planes of perils crossed on tiptoes   finally it is just a split skull into which we stumble but it's how it's split that counts   the clean cut versus the jagged one though sometimes simply softly crushed in the flashing light above a manhole covered by a yellow tent the disheveled foreskin of the head of god a yellow mist surrounds

145. Know not but that who how or what exactly is going on beyond the grave that digs us is something approaching clarity though certainly not ourselves—this means marked by striations where time's folded—keeping going leaping shirts vs. skins vs. animal-vegetable kingdom.

81. Build a bed out of a mattress bought at Hamilton Terrace emporium, a five-by-nine sheet of ¾-inch plywood and saw horses collected off a construction pit on Amsterdam and retire 10-month-old narrow monastic cot you self-imposed without consequence.

11. Try to find the words the wind picks up interlocking yellow leaves scrapping the street, the throat.

148. Awake one morning like in a fairy tale to find yourself with all your paintings and books arrayed and a white cat and a gray cat in a sun-swathed apartment on the top floor of a 20-unit walkup in Brooklyn, a job writing real estate analysis starting in five days, and Kim Jaye, out-of-your-league beautiful, lofty, streaming with grace, expectant with your child, holding you.

bow

there's nothing to see so there's nothing to feel
yellow bough car fender a few houses lit from within
      racing toward hole
            rimmed trails of blood
drag the carcass in
i don't know the whole story
and even its end seems dim
      but i am in it   bow to it

wednesday, march 10, 2000

two blind people walking arm in arm
their eyes a mess talking their sticks
sweeping left right in tandem   some
would posit the one sovereign thing
worth seeing is inside us   move from
describing to feel things climb the
wall built up inside us   most of life
is invisible   most of who we are a
story tapped on the little window

    to come to kindness through the
blindness to feeling through our bod-
ies in all their explosions   on union
square a replica of the labyrinth at
chartes spray painted on the blacktop

39. Know that if it weren't for the fact
that the cats must be fed you
could climb to the stairs at the top
of your head and from there step
out of it.

103. Look again over the west river
from a 13th-floor Starrett Lehigh
loft festooned with palm trees and
women in grass skirts and DJ
playing Burning Spear to new
New Jersey riverside's bristling
power towers.

118. Fall in love.

58. Know snow on the linden branches
toward the sky vanishing.

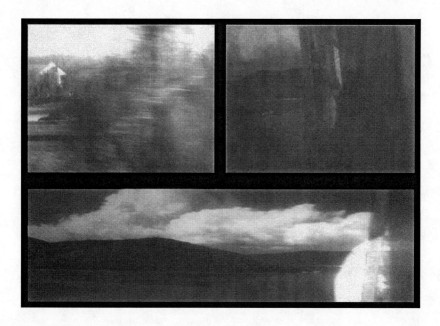

conjunct

              going up the country   going up its ass
that are the trees & leaves that fill its buttocks
        or breasts or bumps along its way
toward feeling or reaching feeling   traveling
to drive to the prize
        to get off   the train   in front of a snow mound
              which is a man in   potentiality
among the banyan trees & busted up forts
& all the crimes in our orange time
        ice in lake scum   blue in sky scum   thought in mind scum
but oddly feeling at this moment
or this string of them just love   tender tuggings
that words have lips

mouth 8

                                    appraise the value of things
                                                of a sky
place your hand in your mouth

rooms
                        laboring up the hill we have come to

                the earth basks as we hasten through the shower
faces shine inwardly building against them
                                    take your foot back and place it
the jungle's drooling thicket the edge of the clearing left toilet
paper purple flowers blue flowers crimson flowers and so i have
come to nothing banging a drum

what is above and what is below
                halting in the stairwell to pick up a curious object
scale does not matter
                            but how to be really   like a golf pro
                                                cool
body with no heart
                                                    elastic
already nothing is left to go inside and die inside
                        anywhere you can make a connection
there are no people
                            an afternoon of sunshine

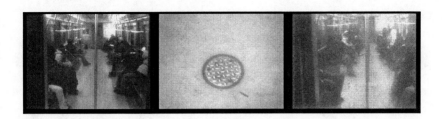

snow

how to become it   separate   salivating   round like suckstone
myth to take to bed to camp
                 along the margin of lives of breaths
which are a euphemism for deaths   as we are for ghosts

blue robin in cuidad de johnson new york park bench where two
                         old-timers hold up
snow on the streets & falling
           just those flakes in window waking on
christina walking in on soula & i moving under covers under
                      snow
as it fell generally over ireland
           separated slathering
if no point no measure   no infinited line
                whatever keeps us strong keeps us ready
nobody is coming in here
           no more boxes to open no more books
no more margins   words in blur in ice open its glass balloon

from one moment to the next we are tethered

sunday, july 12, 1998

—for WD & JB

the skeleton of a single bird on a single tree does
make a spring   backed against memory of these
things concrete wall all is crushed before seen
what is that the pattern of sky as hue heaved in
branches leaves of beech trees sun and now this
one bird and now everything sleeping the grass
its own pillow like words that need no one
around to cut them   the wound is in my eyes
sunsets bruises that guide my heart if i can find
it   famous people walking through the light-
ed room then stand in darkness looking in

warner is sleeping up late left his haake beck
bottle and bali shag cigarette pouch and jim is
sleeping and cherry and flo with a sheet over her
face is sleeping   what happens when you sleep
is your body is alone and all the arrows point
inward toward the same point   the mind a
sheet through which light pours   the raccoon is
not sleeping walks to the edge of the trees and
looks into the house its face like a grandfather

then a grey cat with white back legs walks
where the raccoon was sniffing   molly and nora
are hiding so there is this sphere of silence that is
not made of silence but stillness eyes move in not
breaking as much as weaving it and not tighter
but larger as though to site it it would go on for-
ever   what ideas are being cast around?

what is the logic forms of tongue confound?

a large diamond is buried under the ground i
mean under the ground so that you cannot dig
for it only get there by being the ground and
then lifting yourself off molly's head above the
window sill now looking into the trees in the
direction of where the raccoon was her black fur
glistening

67. Lie in bed with Nora on your chest, head rubbing your chin, listening to her velvet Romanian voice on transatlantic call echoing some secret, deeper Europe, each word formed from her mouth luxuriant as it curls catlike bristling in your ear.

31. Meet her at party on Avenue A to sit with her friends and drink a beer beside an absurd dur-a-flame log fire to then rise together courageously to plunge on and dance through circuit of Lower East Side holes, holding hands and walking through the curiously inspiring-through-contradiction-to-feelings-of-companionship architectural wastes of 3 AM facelessness.

57. Listen on Columbus Circle MTA platform to the cellophane in hands of gorp and potato-chip eaters crinkle in the post-work commute—trains hauling up and away alongside and overhead—that bright crackling sound picked out as M. de Chazal might as a spiked phthalocyanine blue of flowers against jungle canopy.

50. Glimpse Shakespeare in tears standing at the cellar door.

mouth 9

                              triangular message in the 8-ball floating
                                            up like van gogh
there is a god at the top of the stairs

nothing to go through

ways through
   dearest cheeky i lighted this whole matchbook for you slumped
                        over the bar looking up the bartender's nose

                     colder today shorter   like crushed rock
cannot stay. we cannot leave

space that has no face to say what we feel blood drying some
                              and the palaces of eternal space
ochre sky
                        wrapped in a seal skin down by the river
years

to bring the darkness through you in a chain of syllables
11 times the wall
                              periods of funk periods of calm
there is no place to stand

wake

—for AA

at the edge of the woods   what do we know
before going in?
                    like a bulldog   in the woods
          like a leaf on a rock   like a mind on a string
where   a little light is through the trees
                              through the moments
walking on the leaves on the ground
                    with two good looking women
bringing something to birth   bringing nothing to bear
                    how do we dare   go on?
to really be so close to thee   to the earth
               this grace that we were given
to be so close to the earth   to be born
                         even to die to be borne
to feel the earth giving its weight to our own
to feel it all working along walking   feeling
moving   constant rubbing
          the whole of the body the whole of the earth
what weighs more?
something out ahead   broad & white
               something to look forward to
what weighs more   like the dead trees of the forest
like the dead branches of the trees
                         like the dead moments
in our lives
          the little sparks   in the fire
                    into which to throw
          the dead trees of the mind

remembering the smell but not the smell but everything that
                                goes with the smell
who we were how we are   how are you?
how is this ever going to be   more
                            than it is to feel to smell to touch
the rain
            & then to not let go   to not pause
                        to stand at the edge of the lake

thursday, may 27, 1999

or it's raining iridescent mottled frame on earth a film of fuel on the curb only covers so far words or similes or buildings that end in gray the street above the lights to not be on the interstate carrying a bible to be walking under umbrellas anything that is moving between two points two thoughts but maybe not to find something in motion between intervals between cracks everyday to be in love with the cop crouched against the open window of squad car miserable and dark and dim day against towering sky dropping everything crammed into cone watching feet to take aim to take fire

there's just no way that you're gonna to get that bastard

105. Keep yourself separate, heaving the anvil in your chest.

56. Sit to breakfast at the Cherokee Diner amid cabbies and firefighters looking out on morning snow falling before buildings.

122. Write "Harlem Song," viz.

> In my copper town
> love mackle shine shimmy
> home trove bunny bower
>
> no hunger, baby
>
> Come tickle your
> sun shoulder
>
> tangle with the tower
>
> two thongs at night

round

the land is nothing   it can only wait
the ocean is nothing   it can only wait
but where they meet something
                              grows round
bears to be calm & troubled   bears what   emotion
weighs   value of
                    what is a human   heart
what is buried in it   churned in it
grows round   breaks & gathers again
strength that is not its own
only nothing is   feels   something

mouth 10

                       bet against the sunrise and you will lose

feather

                      forward skimming over the pool
terraces of mass and moss nobody is home to tell us how are you
and not to know but be and not to answer the question we are not
enough to figure here fiercer than water

pillars

                         if you remain here i will leave

                    to take a small problem and dissect it
                        coming to terms with polyp

the years

there is a circle outside

                                  wet

                    never look back or ahead

peeked stone

                        "veritable"

guts her whole

                  the man with his arms vs. his eyes
                            crossed

shadows

we have nothing left

note to the reader

The bulk of this book consists of transcriptions of things I spoke into voice recorders: both my early work with audio tape, titled by dates; and a series of audio-visual poems called Transverse made on an Olympus W-10, which allows for photographs to be tied to a sound track and played back as they were taken. The Transverse texts are like scripts with their performances occurring elsewhere, and what I envision is you entering that gap, reading the words from the book while simultaneously listening to the poems online. (Moreover, since many of the original recordings have a  number of photographs that appear in real time, you would also be looking on screen to catch the emerging images, noting the original photos in color are more vivid than their black and white reproduction here.) This bifurcated reading process will allow you to interact more fully with the Transverse series—and best if undertaken on the go, somewhat mirroring the circumstances under which these poems were made. This on-the-go reading can be accomplished via a smart phone, and here's the Quick Response (QR) code for samtruitt.org. Scan the QR code to go to that site, where you will discover more transverse strips (noting some didn't make the migration into *Street Mete*) as well as epexegesis on the book's making.... Discover the mystery of the "1,428 things to do in & around harlem".... Explore what the author made of Thoreau's saying we must be born again to speak what we can write: what it means to fly into that storm a kite.... What the wind picks, the throat, the line made finite as oscillating interval (felt as a throb).... Take measure there of the air building to the right of you building to the left what you think and what you feel among whispers in the structure of at best ambiguous being hard against hulking granite flank of Manhattan Bridge—that keeps us ready.

—*Sam Truitt*

June 2002, photo: Jay Strauss

Sam Truitt is the author of *Vertical Elegies: Three Works, Vertical Elegies 5: The Section, The Song of Rasputin, Anamorphosis Eisenhower,* and *Blazon.* Truitt was born in Washington, DC, and raised there and in Tokyo, Japan, and holds degrees from Kenyon College, Brown University and the University at Albany. He currently teaches in the Language and Thinking Workshop at Bard College and is Managing Director of Station Hill Press in the Hudson Valley, where he lives.

CPSIA information can be obtained at www.ICGtesting.com
Printed in the USA
LVOW070704160911

246410LV00003B/30/P